TREATS

just great recipes

GENERAL INFORMATION

The level of difficulty of the recipes in this book
is expressed as a number from 1 (simple) to 3 (difficult).

TREATS
just great recipes
muffins

McRae Books

MAKES about 12 muffins

PREPARATION 10 min

COOKING 20 min

DIFFICULTY level 1

Apricot Muffins

Preheat the oven to 350°F (180°C/gas 4). • Butter a 12-cup muffin pan. • Sift the flour, baking powder, and salt into a medium bowl. • Beat the eggs, sugar, vanilla, milk, and butter in a large bowl with an electric mixer on medium speed until smooth. • With mixer at low speed, gradually add the dry ingredients, beating until the mixture is smooth and creamy. • Spoon the batter into the prepared pan. Arrange a few slices of apricot on top of each muffin and dust with confectioners' sugar. • Bake until well risen and springy to the touch, about 20 minutes. • Let cool slightly before turning out onto a wire rack. • Dust with the extra confectioners' sugar before serving.

$1\frac{2}{3}$ cups (250 g) all-purpose (plain) flour

2 teaspoons baking powder

$\frac{1}{4}$ teaspoon salt

2 large eggs

$\frac{1}{2}$ cup (100 g) sugar

$\frac{1}{2}$ teaspoon vanilla extract (essence)

1 cup (250 ml) skimmed milk

$\frac{1}{2}$ cup (125 g) butter, melted

4 ripe apricots, pitted and sliced

4 tablespoons confectioners' (icing) sugar + extra, to dust

MAKES about 12 muffins

PREPARATION 15 min

COOKING 25 min

DIFFICULTY level 1

Orange Muffins
with sticky orange sauce

Preheat the oven to 350°F (180°C/gas 4). • Grease a 12-cup muffin pan. • Sift the flour, baking powder, and salt into a medium bowl. Add the almonds and the orange zest and mix well. • Beat the butter, eggs, milk, and half the sugar in a large bowl with an electric mixer on medium speed until smooth. • With mixer at low speed, gradually add the dry ingredients, beating until the mixture is smooth and creamy. • Spoon the batter into the prepared pan. • Bake until well risen and springy to the touch, about 20 minutes. • While the muffins are baking, heat the orange juice and remaining sugar in a small saucepan over low heat. Bring to a boil and simmer until the syrup is reduced by half, about 15 minutes. Remove from the heat and add the liqueur. • Drizzle the hot muffins with the orange syrup. • Let cool slightly before turning out onto a wire rack. • Decorate with orange zest.

2 cups (300 g) all-purpose (plain) flour
2 teaspoons baking powder
$2/3$ cup (60 g) finely ground almonds
Grated zest of 2 large unwaxed oranges
$1/2$ cup (125 g) butter, melted
2 large eggs
1 cup (250 ml) milk
1 cup (200 g) sugar
1 cup (250 ml) fresh orange juice
$1/4$ cup (60 ml) Cointreau or other orange liqueur
Zest of 1 large unwaxed orange, cut into julienne strips

MAKES about 12 muffins

PREPARATION 20 min

COOKING 25 min

DIFFICULTY level 1

Lime Muffins
with yogurt

Preheat the oven to 350°F (180°C/gas 4). • Butter a 12-cup muffin pan. • Grate the zest of 2 limes. Squeeze the juice from 4 limes and thinly slice the remaining lime. • Beat the ricotta, 1 tablespoon of sugar, and 2 tablespoons of the lime juice in a bowl. • Sift the flour baking powder, and salt into a medium bowl. • Beat the eggs, remaining sugar, brown sugar, yogurt, oil, lime zest, and 6 tablespoons of the lime juice in a large bowl with an electric mixer on medium speed until smooth. • With mixer at low speed, gradually add the dry ingredients, beating until the mixture is smooth and creamy. • Spoon half the batter into the cups in the prepared pan. Spoon some of the ricotta mixture into each cup. Cover with the remaining batter. • Bake until well risen and springy to the touch, about 20 minutes. • While the muffins are baking, heat the remaining lime juice with the confectioners' sugar in a small saucepan over low heat. Bring to a boil and add the sliced lime. Simmer until the syrup is slightly thickened and the lime slices are transparent, about 10 minutes Remove from the heat. • Drizzle the hot muffins with the syrup. • Let cool slightly before turning out onto a wire rack. Top with the slices of lime cooked in the syrup.

5 limes

$\frac{1}{2}$ cup (125 g) fresh ricotta cheese, drained

$\frac{3}{4}$ cup (150 g) sugar

$1\frac{2}{3}$ cups (250 g) all-purpose (plain) flour

2 teaspoons baking powder

$\frac{1}{4}$ teaspoon salt

2 large eggs

$\frac{1}{2}$ cup (100 g) firmly packed light brown sugar

Generous $\frac{3}{4}$ cup (200 g) plain yogurt

$\frac{1}{3}$ cup (90 ml) sunflower oil

$\frac{1}{4}$ cup (30 g) confectioners' (icing) sugar

Marbled Muffins

Preheat the oven to 350°F (180°C/gas 4). • Butter a 12-cup muffin pan. • Sift the flour, baking powder, and salt into a small bowl. Stir in the almonds. • Melt the chocolate with half the cream in a double boiler over barely simmering water. • Beat the cocoa, orange zest, and remaining cream in a small bowl. • Beat the eggs, yogurt, butter, and sugar in a large bowl with an electric mixer on medium speed until smooth. • With mixer at low speed, gradually beat in the dry ingredients. • Divide the mixture between two bowls. Add the melted chocolate to one bowl and the cocoa mixture to the other. Place alternate spoonfuls of the light and dark batters in the prepared pan. • Bake until well risen and springy to the touch, about 20 minutes. • Let cool slightly before turning out onto a wire rack.

1 cup (150 g) all-purpose (plain) flour
$2\frac{1}{2}$ teaspoons baking powder
$\frac{1}{4}$ teaspoon salt
1 cup (100 g) finely ground almonds
3 oz (90 g) white chocolate, broken
    into pieces
Generous $\frac{1}{3}$ cup (100 ml) heavy
    (double) cream
2 tablespoons unsweetened cocoa
    powder
Grated zest of $\frac{1}{2}$ orange
2 large eggs
Generous $\frac{3}{4}$ cup (200 g) plain yogurt
$\frac{1}{3}$ cup (90 g) butter, softened
$\frac{1}{2}$ cup (100 g) sugar

Muffins
with prunes and walnuts

Preheat the oven to 350°F (180°C/gas 4). • Butter three 6-cup muffin pans. • Sift the flour, baking powder, cinnamon, and salt into a medium bowl. • Beat the eggs, yogurt, sugar, and oil in a large bowl with an electric mixer on medium speed until smooth. • With mixer at low speed, gradually beat in the dry ingredients. Stir in the coarsely chopped walnuts and prunes. • Spoon the batter into the prepared pans and top each muffin with half a walnut. • Bake until well risen and springy to the touch, about 20 minutes. • Let cool slightly before turning out onto a wire rack.

2 cups (300 g) all-purpose (plain) flour

2 teaspoons baking powder

1 teaspoon ground cinnamon

1/4 teaspoon salt

2 large eggs

1 cup (250 g) plain yogurt

1/2 cup (100 g) firmly packed dark brown sugar

1/3 cup (90 ml) sunflower oil

1 1/4 cups (125 g) coarsely chopped walnuts

8 oz (200 g) prunes, pitted and coarsely chopped

18 walnut halves

MAKES about 12 muffins
PREPARATION 20 min
COOKING 20 min
DIFFICULTY level 1

Jaffa Muffins
with orange liqueur

Preheat the oven to 400°F (200°C/gas 6). • Butter a 12-cup muffin pan. • Melt the chocolate and butter in a double boiler over barely simmering water. • Sift the flour, cocoa, baking powder, and salt into a large bowl. • Stir in the sugar. • Add the eggs, milk, and orange zest, beating with an electric mixer on low speed until well blended. • Beat in the melted chocolate mixture. • Spoon the batter into the prepared pan. • Bake until well risen and springy to the touch, about 20 minutes. • Let cool slightly before turning out onto a wire rack. Let cool completely. • Frosting: Melt the chocolate and butter in a double boiler over barely simmering water. • Remove from the heat and stir in the Cointreau. • Spread the muffins with the frosting. Top with the orange zest and let stand until the frosting has set.

5 oz (150 g) semisweet (dark) chocolate, coarsely chopped
$^1/_3$ cup (90 g) butter
$2^1/_2$ cups (375 g) all-purpose (plain) flour
4 tablespoons unsweetened cocoa powder
2 teaspoons baking powder
$^1/_4$ teaspoon salt
3 tablespoons sugar
2 large eggs
1 cup (250 ml) milk
1 tablespoon finely grated orange zest

Frosting
8 oz (250 g) semisweet (dark) chocolate, chopped
$^1/_4$ cup (60 g) butter
1 tablespoon Cointreau or other orange liqueur
Finely grated orange zest

MAKES about 12 muffins

PREPARATION 15 min

COOKING 20 min

DIFFICULTY level 1

Muffins

with mandarins and chocolate

Set aside 24 mandarin segments for decoration and then chop the rest. • Preheat the oven to 350°F (180°C/gas 4). • Butter a 12-cup muffin pan. • Sift the flour, baking powder, and salt into a medium bowl. • Add the chopped mandarins and chocolate. • Beat the eggs, milk, sugar, and oil in a large bowl with an electric mixer at medium speed until smooth. • With mixer at low speed, gradually beat in the dry ingredients. • Spoon the batter into the prepared pan and then top each muffin with 2 of the reserved mandarin segments. • Bake until well risen and springy to the touch, about 20 minutes. • Let cool slightly before turning out onto a wire rack.

12 oz (350 g) mandarins,
   peeled and divided into segments
2 cups (300 g) all-purpose (plain) flour
2 teaspoons baking powder
1/4 teaspoon salt
5 oz (150 g) yogurt-flavored chocolate,
   coarsely chopped
2 large eggs
1 cup (250 ml) milk
3/4 cup (150 g) sugar
1/3 cup (90 ml) vegetable oil

MAKES about 16 muffins

PREPARATION 15 min

COOKING 20 min

DIFFICULTY level 1

Fruit Muffins
with yogurt

Preheat the oven to 350°F (180°C/gas 4). • Butter three 6-cup muffin pans. • Sift the flour, baking powder, and salt into a medium bowl. • Combine the apples and marmalade in another bowl. • Beat the eggs, yogurt, sugar, and oil in a large bowl with an electric mixer at medium speed. • With mixer at low speed, gradually beat in the dry ingredients until smooth. Stir in the banana. • Half fill the muffin cups with batter. Add a spoonful of the apple and marmalade mixture. Cover with the remaining batter. Sprinkle with sugar crystals. • Bake until well risen and springy to the touch, about 20 minutes. • Let cool slightly before turning out onto a wire rack.

2 cups (300 g) all-purpose (plain) flour
2 teaspoons baking powder
1/4 teaspoon salt
3 ripe apples, peeled, cored, and grated
2/3 cup (200 g) orange marmalade
2 large eggs
Generous 3/4 cup (200 g) plain yogurt
1/2 cup (100 g) sugar
1/3 cup (90 ml) vegetable oil
1 large ripe banana, mashed
2 tablespoons sugar crystals

13

MAKES about 12 muffins

PREPARATION 15 min

COOKING 20 min

DIFFICULTY level 1

Coconut Muffins
with chocolate and rum

Preheat the oven to 350°F (180°C/gas 4). • Butter a 12-cup muffin pan. • Beat the coconut and ½ cup (125 ml) of the rum in a small bowl. • Sift the flour, cocoa, baking powder, and salt into a medium bowl. • Place the butter and milk in a saucepan over low heat and stir until the butter has melted. Remove from the heat. • Beat the eggs and sugar in a large bowl with an electric mixer at high speed until pale and creamy. • With mixer at low speed, gradually beat in the butter, milk, and coconut mixture, alternating with the dry ingredients. Spoon the batter into the prepared pan. • Bake until well risen and springy to the touch, about 20 minutes. • Let cool slightly before turning out onto a wire rack. Let cool completely. • Melt the chocolate with the remaining rum in a double boiler over barely simmering water. Spread each muffin with the frosting.

Scant ⅔ cup (75 g) shredded (desiccated) coconut
⅔ cup (150 ml) rum
1 cup (150 g) all-purpose (plain) flour
⅓ cup (50 g) unsweetened cocoa powder
2 teaspoons baking powder
¼ teaspoon salt
½ cup (125 g) butter, melted
1 cup (250 ml) milk
2 large eggs
¾ cup (150 g) sugar
6 oz (180 g) milk chocolate, broken into pieces

MAKES about 12 muffins
PREPARATION 15 min
COOKING 25 min
DIFFICULTY level 2

Blueberry Muffins
with white chocolate

Preheat the oven to 350°F (180°C/gas 4). • Butter a 12-cup muffin pan. • Sift the flour, baking powder, and salt into a medium bowl. • Melt 5 oz (150 g) of the chocolate with the milk in a double boiler over barely simmering water. • Beat the eggs, sugar, vanilla, butter, and melted chocolate mixture in a large bowl with an electric mixer at medium speed until smooth. • With mixer at low speed, gradually beat in the dry ingredients. • Stir the blueberries in by hand. • Spoon the batter into the prepared pan. • Bake until well risen and springy to the touch, about 20 minutes. • Let cool slightly before turning out onto a wire rack. Let cool completely. • Melt the remaining chocolate in a double boiler over barely simmering water. • Drizzle the melted chocolate over the muffins.

$1\frac{2}{3}$ cups (250 g) all-purpose (plain) flour
2 teaspoons baking powder
$\frac{1}{4}$ teaspoon salt
8 oz (250 g) white chocolate, broken into pieces
Generous $\frac{3}{4}$ cup (200 ml) milk
2 large eggs
$\frac{1}{2}$ cup (100 g) sugar
$\frac{1}{2}$ teaspoon vanilla extract (essence)
$\frac{1}{3}$ cup (90 g) butter, softened
8 oz (250 g) frozen blueberries, thawed

MAKES about 12 muffins

PREPARATION 15 min

COOKING 20 min

DIFFICULTY level 1

Muffins

with coconut and cranberry

Preheat the oven to 350°F (180°C/gas 4). • Butter a 12-cup muffin pan. • Melt the chocolate with the milk in a double boiler over barely simmering water. Remove from the heat and let cool. • Sift the flour, baking powder, and salt into a medium bowl. Stir in the cranberries and coconut. • Beat the eggs, sugar, and oil in a large bowl with an electric mixer on medium speed until smooth. • With mixer on low, gradually beat in the dry ingredients and melted chocolate mixture. • Spoon the batter into the prepared pan. • Bake until well risen and springy to the touch, about 20 minutes. • Let cool slightly before turning out onto a wire rack.

4 oz (125 g) white chocolate, broken into pieces

1 cup (250 ml) milk

1⅔ cups (250 g) all-purpose (plain) flour

2 teaspoons baking powder

¼ teaspoon salt

5 oz (150 g) dried cranberries

½ cup (50 g) shredded (desiccated) coconut

2 large eggs

½ cup (100 g) sugar

⅓ cup (90 ml) sunflower oil

MAKES about 12 muffins

PREPARATION 15 min

COOKING 20 min

DIFFICULTY level 1

Muffins
with caramel sauce

Preheat the oven to 350°F (180°C/gas 4). • Butter a 12-cup muffin pan. • Sift the flour, baking powder, and salt into a medium bowl. • Beat the eggs, butter, sugar, caramel flavoring, and milk in a large bowl with an electric mixer on medium speed until smooth. • With mixer on low, gradually beat in the dry ingredients. • Spoon the batter into the prepared pan. • Bake until well risen and springy to the touch, about 20 minutes. • Let cool slightly before turning out onto a wire rack. Top with caramel sauce before serving.

2 cups (300 g) all-purpose (plain) flour
2 teaspoons baking powder
1/4 teaspoon salt
2 large eggs
1/2 cup (100 g) butter, melted
3/4 cup (150 g) sugar
2 tablespoons caramel flavoring
1 cup (250 ml) milk
1/3 cup (90 ml) ready-made caramel sauce

MAKES about 12 muffins
PREPARATION 20 min
COOKING 20 min
DIFFICULTY level 2

Chocolate Muffins
with cherry and port topping

Preheat the oven to 375°F (190°C/gas 5). • Butter a 12-cup muffin pan. • Melt the chocolate and butter in a double boiler over barely simmering water. Remove from the heat and let cool. • Sift the flour, baking powder, and salt into a medium bowl. • Beat the eggs, sugar, and vanilla in a large bowl with an electric mixer on medium speed until pale and creamy. • With mixer on low, gradually beat in the dry ingredients and the melted chocolate mixture. • Spoon half the batter into the prepared pan. Place two chopped cherries in each muffin and top with the remaining batter. • Bake until well risen and springy to the touch, about 20 minutes. • Let cool slightly before turning out onto a wire rack. • Cherry Topping: Place the cornstarch in a small bowl and stir in the port until smooth. • Place the cherries and sugar in a medium saucepan over low heat. Stir in the port mixture and simmer for 10 minutes. • Decorate the cooled muffins with the cherry topping just before serving.

5 oz (150 g) semisweet (dark) chocolate, coarsely chopped
½ cup (125 g) butter
1⅔ cups (250 g) all-purpose (plain) flour
2 teaspoons baking powder
¼ teaspoon salt
¾ cup (150 g) sugar
2 large eggs
1 teaspoon vanilla extract (essence)
24 fresh cherries, pitted and coarsely chopped

Cherry Topping
1 teaspoon cornstarch (cornflour)
½ cup (125 ml) white port
8 oz (250) g fresh cherries, with stalks
½ cup (100 g) sugar

20

MAKES about 12 muffins

PREPARATION 20 min

COOKING 20 min

DIFFICULTY level 2

Muffins
with ginger, pear, and chocolate

Place the pears in a bowl with 1 tablespoon of the syrup from the ginger and mix well. Drain the ginger and chop very finely. • Preheat the oven to 350°F (180°C/gas 4). • Butter a 12-cup muffin pan. • Sift the flour, baking powder, and salt into a medium bowl. Stir in the walnuts and the cocoa. • Beat the eggs and sugar in a large bowl with an electric mixer on high speed until pale and creamy. • With mixer on low speed, gradually add the butter and milk alternating with the dry ingredients and beating until smooth. • Stir in the ginger and pears by hand. • Spoon the batter into the prepared pan. • Bake until well risen and springy to the touch, about 20 minutes. • Let cool slightly before turning out onto a wire rack. Let cool completely. • Melt the white chocolate in a double boiler over barely simmering water. Drizzle the melted chocolate over the muffins. Top each muffin with a walnut half. Let cool completely before serving.

2 large ripe pears, peeled, cored, and cut into small cubes

2 oz (60 g) stem ginger preserved in syrup, with syrup

1²⁄₃ cups (250 g) all-purpose (plain) flour

2¹⁄₂ teaspoons baking powder

¹⁄₄ teaspoon salt

³⁄₄ cup (75 g) chopped walnuts

2 tablespoons unsweetened cocoa powder

2 large eggs

¹⁄₂ cup (100 g) sugar

¹⁄₂ cup (100 g) butter, softened

1 cup (250 ml) milk

4 oz (125 g) white chocolate

12 walnut halves, to decorate

MAKES about 12 muffins

PREPARATION 20 min

COOKING 20 min

DIFFICULTY level 1

Muffins

with chocolate and chile

Preheat the oven to 350°F (180°C/gas 4). • Butter a 12-cup muffin pan. • Melt the chocolate and butter in a double boiler over barely simmering water. Set aside to cool. • Sift the flour, cocoa, baking powder, chile, and salt into a medium bowl. Stir in the almonds. • Beat the eggs, sugar, and milk in a large bowl with an electric mixer on medium speed until smooth. • With mixer on low speed, gradually beat in the dry ingredients, alternating with the chocolate and butter mixture. • Spoon the batter into the prepared pan. • Bake until well risen and springy to the touch, about 20 minutes. • Let cool slightly before turning out onto a wire rack. Let cool completely. • Decorate each muffin with a little whipped cream and a pinch of chile powder.

4 oz (125 g) bittersweet (dark) chocolate, broken into pieces
$\frac{1}{2}$ cup (125 g) butter
1 cup (150 g) all-purpose (plain) flour
2 tablespoons unsweetened cocoa powder
2 teaspoons baking powder
1 teaspoon chile powder
$\frac{1}{4}$ teaspoon salt
$1\frac{1}{4}$ cups (125 g) finely ground almonds
2 large eggs
$\frac{1}{2}$ cup (100 g) sugar
1 cup (250 ml) milk

To Decorate
1 cup (250 ml) whipped cream
$\frac{1}{2}$ teaspoon chile powder

MAKES about 12 muffins

PREPARATION 20 min

COOKING 20 min

DIFFICULTY level 1

Muffins
with apricot and almonds

Preheat the oven to 350°F (180°C/gas 4). • Butter a 12-cup muffin pan. • Sift the flour, baking powder, and salt into a medium bowl. • Place the almonds, apricots, marzipan, and orange juice in a blender and chop to make a smooth paste. • Beat the eggs, sugar, orange zest, milk, and oil, in a large bowl with an electric mixer on medium speed until smooth. • With mixer on low speed, gradually add the dry ingredients, beating until smooth. • Spoon half the batter into the prepared pan. Spoon part of the orange and almond mixture into each cup. Cover with the remaining batter. • Bake until well risen and springy to the touch, about 20 minutes. • Let cool slightly before turning out onto a wire rack.

1⅔ cups (250 g) all-purpose (plain) flour
2½ teaspoons baking powder
¼ teaspoon salt
½ cup (50 g) finely ground almonds
Generous ½ cup (100 g) chopped dried apricots
4 oz (125 g) marzipan, cut into small cubes
Generous ⅓ cup (100 ml) fresh orange juice
2 large eggs
½ cup (100 g) sugar
Grated zest of 1 large orange
1 cup (250 ml) milk
⅓ cup (90 ml) vegetable oil

MAKES about 12 muffins

PREPARATION 15 min

COOKING 20 min

DIFFICULTY level 1

Nutty Muffins
with yogurt and spice

Preheat the oven to 350°F (180°C/gas 4). • Butter a 12-cup muffin pan. • Sift the flour, baking powder, cinnamon, ginger, and salt into a medium bowl. Stir in the raisins, hazelnuts, and candied lemon peel. • Beat the eggs, yogurt, and sugar in a large bowl with an electric mixer on medium speed until smooth. • With mixer on low speed, gradually beat in the dry ingredients and butter. • Spoon the mixture into the prepared pan. Top each muffin with 3 almonds. • Bake until well risen and springy to the touch, about 20 minutes. • Let cool slightly before turning out onto a wire rack.

1 cup (150 g) all-purpose (plain) flour
2$\frac{1}{2}$ teaspoons baking powder
1 teaspoon ground cinnamon
1 teaspoon ground ginger
$\frac{1}{4}$ teaspoon salt
$\frac{1}{2}$ cup (75 g) raisins
1 cup (100 g) finely ground hazelnuts
$\frac{1}{2}$ cup (75 g) candied lemon peel, chopped
2 large eggs
1 cup (250 ml) plain yogurt
$\frac{1}{2}$ cup (100 g) sugar
$\frac{1}{2}$ cup (125 g) butter, melted
36 blanched almonds

Aniseed Muffins
with pine nuts

Preheat the oven to 350°F (180°C/gas 4). • Butter a 12-cup muffin pan. • Sift the flour, baking powder, and salt into a medium bowl. Stir in the pine nuts and 2 teaspoons of aniseed. • Beat the eggs, sugar, oil, and milk in a large bowl with an electric mixer on medium speed until smooth. • With mixer on low speed, gradually beat in the dry ingredients. • Spoon the batter into the prepared pan. • Bake until well risen and springy to the touch, about 20 minutes. • Let cool slightly before turning out onto a wire rack. Let cool completely. • Beat the confectioners' sugar, lemon juice, and remaining aniseed in a small bowl. • Spread the muffins with this mixture.

$1^2/_3$ cups (250 g) all-purpose (plain) flour

$2^1/_2$ teaspoons baking powder

$^1/_4$ teaspoon salt

Generous $^1/_2$ cup (100 g) pine nuts

3 teaspoons ground aniseed

2 large eggs

$^1/_2$ cup (100 g) sugar

$^1/_3$ cup (90 ml) vegetable oil

1 cup (250 ml) milk

1 cup (150 g) confectioners' (icing) sugar

2 tablespoons lemon juice

Muffins

with cashews and pears

Place the chopped pears in a medium bowl with the lemon juice and mix well. • Preheat the oven to 350°F (180°C/gas 4). • Butter a 12-cup muffin pan. • Sift the flour, baking powder, and salt into a medium bowl. Stir in the cashews. • Beat the eggs, sugar, oil, and milk in a large bowl with an electric mixer on medium speed until smooth. • With mixer on low speed, gradually beat in the dry ingredients and pear mixture. • Spoon the batter into the prepared pan. • Bake until well risen and springy to the touch, about 20 minutes. • Let cool slightly before turning out onto a wire rack. • Dust with confectioners' sugar just before serving.

3 large ripe pears, peeled, cored and chopped

2 tablespoons fresh lemon juice

1²/₃ cups (250 g) all-purpose (plain) flour

2¹/₂ teaspoons baking powder

¹/₄ teaspoon salt

1 cup (100 g) finely chopped cashew nuts

2 large eggs

¹/₂ cup (100 g) sugar

¹/₃ cup (90 ml) sunflower oil

1 cup (250 ml) milk

4 tablespoons confectioners' (icing) sugar, to dust

MAKES about 20 muffins

PREPARATION 15 min

COOKING 20 min

DIFFICULTY level 1

Muffins

with pears and pecans

Preheat the oven to 350°F (180°C/gas 4). • Butter two 12-cup muffin pans. • Sift the flour, baking powder, cinnamon, nutmeg, and salt into a large bowl. • Stir in the brown sugar, chopped pecans, and pears. • Add the eggs, milk, and vanilla and beat with an electric mixer on medium speed until well blended. • Stir in the butter. • Spoon the batter into the prepared cups. Top each muffin with half a pecan. • Bake until well risen and springy to the touch, about 20 minutes. • Let cool slightly before turning out onto a wire rack. • Dust with the confectioners' sugar just before serving.

3 cups (450 g) all-purpose (plain) flour
2 teaspoons baking powder
1 teaspoon ground cinnamon
1/2 teaspoon freshly grated nutmeg
1/4 teaspoon salt
1/2 cup (100 g) firmly packed
    brown sugar
1 cup (100 g) chopped pecans, toasted
14 oz (400 g) firm-ripe pears, peeled,
    cored, and thinly sliced
2 large eggs
1 1/2 cups (375 ml) milk
1 teaspoon vanilla extract (essence)
1/2 cup (125 g) butter
10 pecan nuts, cut in half, to decorate
6 tablespoons confectioners' (icing)
    sugar, to dust

Rose Muffins

with almonds

Preheat the oven to 350°F (180°C/gas 4). • Butter a 12-cup muffin pan. • Sift the flour, baking powder, and salt into a medium bowl. Stir in the almonds. • Beat the eggs, yogurt, half the sugar, and the oil in a large bowl with an electric mixer at medium speed until smooth. • With mixer on low speed, gradually beat in the dry ingredients. • Spoon the batter into the prepared pan. • Bake until well risen and springy to the touch, about 20 minutes. • Let cool slightly before turning out onto a wire rack. • Place the remaining sugar and the water in a small saucepan over low heat and bring to a boil. Simmer until the syrup is slightly reduced, 3–4 minutes. Remove from the heat and let cool. Add the rose water and lemon juice and mix well. • Drizzle the muffins with the rose syrup and then let cool completely. • Dissolve the confectioners' sugar in 1–2 teaspoons of boiling water in a small bowl. Drizzle this mixture over the muffins and then decorate with rose petals.

1 1/3 cups (200 g) all-purpose (plain) flour

3 teaspoons baking powder

1/4 teaspoon salt

1/2 cup (50 g) finely ground almonds

2 large eggs

Scant 1 1/4 cups (300 g) plain yogurt

1 cup (200 g) sugar

1/3 cup (90 ml) vegetable oil

1/3 cup (90 ml) water

1/4 cup (60 ml) rose water

1/4 cup (60 ml) lemon juice

1/3 cup (50 g) confectioners' (icing) sugar

Crystallized rose petals, to decorate

Ginger Muffins
with orange marmalade

Preheat the oven to 350°F (180°C/gas 4). • Butter a 12-cup muffin pan. • Sift the flour, baking powder, and salt into a medium bowl. Stir in the lemon zest. • Beat the eggs, sugar, cream, milk, lemon juice, and butter in a large bowl with an electric mixer on medium speed until smooth. • With mixer on low speed, gradually beat in the dry ingredients. • Spoon the batter into the prepared pan. • Bake until well risen and springy to the touch, about 20 minutes. • Let cool slightly before turning out onto a wire rack. • Melt the marmalade in a small saucepan over low heat. Brush the muffins with the marmalade just before serving.

$1^2/_3$ cups (250 g) all-purpose (plain) flour

$2^1/_2$ teaspoons baking powder

$1/_4$ teaspoon salt

Finely grated zest of 1 lemon

2 large eggs,

$1/_2$ cup (100 g) sugar

$1/_2$ cup (125 ml) heavy (double) cream

$1/_2$ cup (125 ml) milk

Freshly squeezed juice of 1 lemon

$2/_3$ cup (150 g) butter, melted

3 oz (90 g) stem ginger preserved in syrup, drained and chopped

4 tablespoons orange marmalade

MAKES about 12 muffins

PREPARATION 20 min

COOKING 20 min

DIFFICULTY level 1

Apple Muffins
with raisins and ricotta cheese

Place the apples in a medium bowl with the lemon zest and juice. Mix well. • Preheat the oven to 350°F (180°C/gas 4). • Butter a 12-cup muffin pan. • Sift the flour, baking powder, and salt into a medium bowl. Stir in the raisins. • Beat the ricotta, milk, sugar, eggs, and butter in a large bowl with an electric mixer at medium speed until smooth. • With mixer on low speed, gradually beat in the dry ingredients and apple mixture. • Spoon the batter into the prepared pan. • Bake until well risen and springy to the touch, about 25 minutes. • Let cool slightly before turning out onto a wire rack. • Dust with the confectioners' sugar just before serving.

3 large ripe apples,
   peeled, cored, and grated
Finely grated zest and juice of 1 lemon
1²⁄₃ cups (250 g) all-purpose (plain)
   flour
2¹⁄₂ teaspoons baking powder
¹⁄₄ teaspoon salt
Generous ¹⁄₂ cup (100 g) raisins
1 cup (250 g) ricotta cheese, drained
²⁄₃ cup (150 ml) milk
¹⁄₂ cup (100 g) sugar
2 large eggs
¹⁄₂ cup (125 g) butter, melted
4 tablespoons confectioners' (icing)
   sugar

MAKES about 12 muffins

PREPARATION 10 min

COOKING 20 min

DIFFICULTY level 1

Carrot Muffins
with pine nuts

Preheat the oven to 375°F (190°C/gas 5). • Butter a 12-cup muffin pan. • Sift the flour, baking powder, and salt into a medium bowl. Stir in the pine nuts. • Beat the confectioners' sugar and butter in a large bowl with an electric mixer at high speed until pale and creamy. • With mixer at medium speed, add the egg yolks one at a time, beating until just combined after each addition. • With mixer on low speed, gradually add the dry ingredients and carrots, beating until smooth. • Beat the egg whites in a large bowl with mixer at high speed until stiff peaks form. Fold the whites into the batter. • Spoon the batter into the prepared pan. • Bake until well risen and springy to the touch, about 20 minutes. • Let cool slightly before turning out onto a wire rack. • Dust with the confectioners' sugar just before serving.

8 oz (250 g) finely grated carrots

1²⁄₃ cups (250 g) all-purpose (plain) flour

1¹⁄₂ teaspoons baking powder

¹⁄₄ teaspoon salt

¹⁄₂ cup (100 g) finely chopped pine nuts

²⁄₃ cup (100 g) confectioners' (icing) sugar + extra, to dust

³⁄₄ cup (180 g) butter

4 large eggs + 1 large egg yolk

MAKES about 12 muffins

PREPARATION 30 min

COOKING 30 min

DIFFICULTY level 2

Dessert Muffins
with chocolate and tropical coulis

Preheat the oven to 350°F (180°C/gas 4). • Butter a 12-cup muffin pan. • Sift the flour, potato starch, and baking powder into a large bowl. • Beat the butter and ⅔ cup (100 g) of confectioners' sugar in a large bowl with an electric mixer on medium speed until pale and creamy. • Add the ginger, egg, and egg yolks, beating until just blended. • With mixer on low speed, gradually add the chocolate and dry ingredients to make a smooth batter. • Spoon the batter into the prepared cups. • Bake until well risen and springy to the touch, about 20 minutes. • Let cool slightly before turning out onto a wire rack. Let cool completely. • Chocolate Sauce: Melt the chocolate and cream in a double boiler over barely simmering water. • Tropical Coulis: Place the mango, papaya, passionfruit, sugar, and rum in a food processor or blender and chop until smooth. • Place the warm muffins on serving dishes. • Spoon a little of each sauce onto the dishes around the base of the muffins. Dust with the confectioners' sugar and sprinkle with the almonds. Garnish with the whipped cream and serve.

⅓ cup (50 g) all-purpose (plain) flour
2 tablespoons potato starch
1 teaspoon baking powder
⅓ cup (90 g) butter
1 cup (150 g) confectioners' (icing) sugar
1 tablespoon fresh minced ginger
1 large egg + 3 large egg yolks
2 oz (60 g) semisweet chocolate, melted

Chocolate Sauce
4 oz (125 g) bittersweet chocolate, coarsely chopped
½ cup (125 ml) heavy (double) cream

Tropical Coulis
4 oz (125 g) mango, peeled and coarsely chopped
4 oz (125 g) papaya, peeled and seeded
1 passionfruit, pulped and strained
⅓ cup (75 g) sugar
2 tablespoons dark rum

Confectioners' (icing) sugar, to dust
Flaked almonds, to decorate
Whipped cream, to serve

MAKES about 12 muffins

PREPARATION 15 min

COOKING 20 min

DIFFICULTY level 1

Rice Muffins

Preheat the oven to 350°F (180°C/gas 4). • Butter a 12-cup muffin pan. • Sift the flour, baking powder, and salt into a large bowl. • Add the eggs one at a time, beating with an electric mixer on medium speed until just blended after each addition. • With mixer on low, add the milk, butter, sugar, rum, and salt, beating until smooth. • Stir in the rice. • Spoon the batter into the prepared pan. • Bake until well risen and springy to the touch, about 20 minutes. • Let cool slightly before turning out onto a wire rack. • Dust with the confectioners' sugar just before serving.

1 cup (150 g) all-purpose (plain) flour
1 teaspoon baking powder
1/4 teaspoon salt
3 large eggs
1 cup (250 ml) milk
1/4 cup (60 g) butter, melted
2 tablespoons sugar
1 tablespoon rum
1/2 teaspoon salt
1 cup (75 g) boiled rice
1/3 cup (50 g) confectioners' (icing) sugar, to dust

MAKES about 18 muffins

PREPARATION 20 min

COOKING 20 min

DIFFICULTY level 1

Muffins

with cherries and almonds

Preheat the oven to 350°F (180°C/gas 4). • Butter three 6-cup muffin pans. • Sift the flour, baking powder, and salt into a large bowl. • Beat the butter, 1 cup (200 g) of sugar, and almond extract in a large bowl with an electric mixer at medium speed until creamy. • Add the eggs one at a time, beating until just blended after each addition. • With mixer at low speed, gradually beat in the dry ingredients, alternating with the milk. • Stir in the cherries and almonds. • Spoon the batter into the prepared pans. Sprinkle with the remaining sugar • Bake until well risen and springy to the touch, about 20 minutes. • Let cool slightly before turning out onto a wire rack.

2 cups (300 g) all-purpose (plain) flour
2 teaspoons baking powder
1/4 teaspoon salt
1/2 cup (125 g) butter
1 1/4 cups (250 g) sugar
1/2 teaspoon almond extract (essence)
2 large eggs
1/2 cup (125 ml) milk
2 cups (200 g) canned cherries, drained, pitted, and coarsely chopped
1 cup (75 g) coarsely chopped almonds, lightly toasted

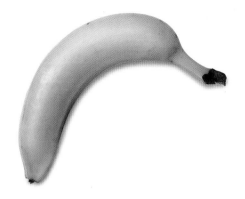

MAKES about 18 muffins

PREPARATION 15 min

COOKING 20 min

DIFFICULTY level 1

Banana Muffins
with chocolate chips

Preheat the oven to 350°F (180°C/gas 4). • Butter three 6-cup muffin pans. • Sift both flours, baking powder, baking soda, and salt into a large bowl. • Beat the butter and sugar in a large bowl with an electric mixer at medium speed until creamy. • Add the eggs one at a time, beating until just blended after each addition. • With mixer on low, beat in the bananas, followed by the dry ingredients, alternating with the milk. • Stir in the chocolate chips and walnuts by hand. • Spoon the batter into the prepared pans. • Bake until well risen and springy to the touch, about 20 minutes. • Let cool slightly before turning out onto a wire rack.

1 cup (150 g) whole-wheat (wholemeal) flour
1 cup (150 g) all-purpose (plain) flour
2 teaspoons baking powder
1/2 teaspoon baking soda
1/4 teaspoon salt
1/2 cup (125 g) butter
1 cup (200 g) sugar
3 large eggs
2 large very ripe bananas, mashed with a fork
1/4 cup (60 ml) milk
1 cup (180 g) semisweet chocolate chips
1 cup (100 g) walnuts, chopped

MAKES about 12 muffins
PREPARATION 30 min
COOKING 20 min
DIFFICULTY level 2

Muffins
with passionfruit and mango

Preheat the oven to 350°F (180°C/gas 4). • Butter a 12-cup muffin pan. • Sift the flour, baking powder, baking soda, and salt into a large bowl. • Beat the butter and sugar in a large bowl with an electric mixer at medium speed until creamy. • Add the eggs, one at a time, beating until just blended after each addition. • With mixer at low speed, gradually beat in the dry ingredients, alternating with the cream. • Stir in the mango and passionfruit pulp. • Spoon the batter into the prepared cups. • Bake until well risen and springy to the touch, about 20 minutes. • Let cool slightly before turning out onto a wire rack. Let cool completely. • Yogurt Cream: With mixer at high speed, beat the cream and yogurt in a medium bowl until stiff. Fold in the lemon zest and passion fruit pulp. • Cut a small "hat" from the top of each muffin. Fill with the cream and top with the "hat."

2 cups (300 g) all-purpose (plain) flour
2 teaspoons baking powder
$1/2$ teaspoon baking soda
$1/4$ teaspoon salt
$1/2$ cup (125 g) butter, softened
$3/4$ cup (150 g) sugar
2 large eggs
$1/2$ cup (125 ml) heavy (double) cream
$1/2$ cup (60 g) finely chopped candied mango
4 tablespoons fresh passionfruit pulp

Yogurt Cream
$1/2$ cup (125 ml) heavy (double) cream
$1/2$ cup (125 ml) plain yogurt
2 teaspoons finely grated lemon zest
1 tablespoon fresh passionfruit pulp

MAKES about 12 muffins

PREPARATION 25 min

COOKING 30 min

DIFFICULTY level 1

Muffins

with strawberry sauce

Preheat the oven to 350°F (180°C/gas 4). • Butter a 12-cup muffin pan. • Sift both flours, the baking powder, and salt into a medium bowl. • Beat the butter and sugar in a large bowl with an electric mixer at medium speed until creamy. • Add the eggs, one at a time, beating until just blended after each addition. • With mixer at low speed, gradually beat in the dry ingredients, alternating with the milk. • Spoon the batter into the prepared cups. • Bake until well risen and springy to the touch, about 20 minutes. • Let cool slightly before turning out onto a wire rack. • Strawberry Sauce: Melt the butter in a medium saucepan over low heat. Add the strawberries and sugar and simmer until the strawberries have broken down, about 15 minutes. • Spoon over the muffins and serve warm.

1 cup (150 g) all-purpose (plain) flour
1 cup (150 g) whole-wheat (wholemeal) flour
2 teaspoons baking powder
1/4 teaspoon salt
1/3 cup (90 g) butter
1/2 cup (100 g) sugar
1 cup (250 ml) milk
2 large eggs

Strawberry Sauce
3 tablespoons butter
1 lb (500 g) strawberries
1/3 cup (75 g) sugar

MAKES about 12 muffins

PREPARATION 15 min

COOKING 20 min

DIFFICULTY level 1

Muffins
with honey and thyme

Preheat the oven to 350°F (180°C/gas 4). • Butter a 12-cup muffin pan. • Sift the flour, baking powder, and salt into a medium bowl. Stir in the almonds and thyme. • Beat the eggs, honey, 3 tablespoons of the demerara sugar, butter, and milk in a large bowl with an electric mixer at medium speed until smooth. • With mixer on low, gradually beat in the dry ingredients. • Spoon the batter into the prepared pan and sprinkle with the remaining sugar. • Bake until well risen and springy to the touch, about 20 minutes. • Let cool slightly before turning out onto a wire rack.

1 cup (150 g) all-purpose (plain) flour
1½ teaspoons baking powder
¼ teaspoon salt
1 tablespoon finely chopped thyme
1 cup (100 g) finely ground almonds
2 large eggs
½ cup (125 g) clear honey
⅓ cup (70 g) demerara or raw sugar
Generous ⅓ cup (90 g) butter, softened
1 cup (250 ml) milk

MAKES about 18 muffins

PREPARATION 15 min

COOKING 20 min

DIFFICULTY level 1

Zucchini Muffins
with lime frosting

Preheat the oven to 350°F (180°C/gas 4). • Butter three 6-cup muffin pans. • Sift the flour, baking powder, baking soda, and salt into a large bowl. Stir in the brown sugar, lemon zest, walnuts, and raisins. • Beat the eggs, oil, lime juice, and milk in a large bowl with an electric mixer on medium speed until smooth. Stir the egg mixture into the dry ingredients. Fold in the zucchini. • Spoon the batter into the prepared cups. • Bake until well risen and springy to the touch, about 20 minutes. • Let cool slightly before turning out onto a wire rack. Let cool completely. • Lime Frosting: Beat the cream cheese and confectioners' sugar in a bowl with an electric mixer at medium speed until creamy. Beat in the lime zest and enough juice to make a thick, spreadable frosting. • Spread the frosting over the cooled muffins.

2 cups (300 g) all-purpose (plain) flour
2 teaspoons baking powder
1 teaspoon baking soda
1/4 teaspoon salt
1/2 cup (100 g) firmly packed brown sugar
1 tablespoon finely grated lemon zest
1 cup (75 g) chopped walnuts
1/2 cup (180 g) raisins
2 large eggs
1/3 cup (90 ml) vegetable oil
1/4 cup (60 ml) lime juice
1/4 cup (60 ml) milk
1 cup (200 g) firmly packed shredded zucchini

Lime Frosting
3 oz (90 g) cream cheese
1 cup (150 g) confectioners' (icing) sugar
1 tablespoon finely grated lime zest
1 tablespoon fresh lime juice

MAKES about 12 muffins

PREPARATION 15 min

COOKING 30 min

DIFFICULTY level 1

Muffins
with bacon and hazelnuts

Preheat the oven to 375°F (190°C/gas 5). • Butter a 12-cup muffin pan. • Sauté the bacon in a large frying pan over medium heat until lightly browned, 3–4 minutes. • Add the onion and hazelnuts and sauté until the onion is tender, 3–4 minutes. • Sift the flour, baking powder, and salt into a medium bowl. • Beat the eggs, butter, yogurt, and milk in a large bowl with an electric mixer on medium speed. • With mixer on low speed, add the bacon mixture and the dry ingredients, beating until just combined. • Spoon the batter into the prepared pan. • Bake until well risen and springy to the touch, about 20 minutes. • Let cool slightly before turning out onto a wire rack.

8 oz (250 g) chopped bacon, finely chopped
1 small onion, finely chopped
1/2 cup (50 g) finely chopped hazelnuts
1 1/2 cups (225 g) all-purpose (plain) flour
3 teaspoons baking powder
1/2 teaspoon salt
2 large eggs
1/3 cup (90 g) butter, melted
1/2 cup (125 ml) plain yogurt
Generous 3/4 cup (200 ml) milk

Muffins

with carrots and goat cheese

Preheat the oven to 350°F (180°C/gas 4). • Butter three 6-cup muffin pans. • Sift the flour, baking powder, and salt into a medium bowl. • Beat the eggs in a large bowl with an electric mixer on medium speed. Add the yogurt, oil, cumin, coriander, and pepper. • With mixer on low speed, add the dry ingredients, grated cheese, carrots, and cilantro, beating until just combined. • Place the goat cheese into a small bowl and mix using a fork to make a smooth cream. Stir into the batter by hand. • Spoon the batter into the prepared pan. • Bake until well risen and springy to the touch, about 20 minutes. • Let cool slightly before turning out onto a wire rack.

2 cups (300 g) all-purpose (plain) flour
2 teaspoons baking powder
$1/4$ teaspoon salt
3 large eggs
1 cup (250 ml) natural yogurt
$1/4$ cup (60 ml) extra-virgin olive oil
1 teaspoon ground coriander
$1/2$ teaspoon ground cumin
Freshly ground black pepper
4 oz (125 g) Gruyère, coarsely grated
3 medium carrots, peeled and grated
1 tablespoon finely chopped cilantro (coriander)
8 oz (250 g) fresh creamy goat cheese

Muffins

with ham, peas, and corn

Preheat the oven to 350°F (180°C/gas 4). • Butter a 12-cup muffin pan. • Sift the flour, baking powder, salt, and pepper into a bowl. Stir in the Parmesan. • Beat the eggs, butter, and milk in a large bowl with an electric mixer on medium speed. • With mixer on low speed, add the peas, corn, ham and dry ingredients, beating until just combined. • Spoon the batter into the prepared pan. • Bake until well risen and springy to the touch, about 20 minutes. • Let cool slightly before turning out onto a wire rack.

2 cups (300 g) all-purpose (plain) flour
2 teaspoons baking powder
1/2 teaspoon salt
1/2 teaspoon freshly ground black pepper
6 tablespoons freshly grated Parmesan
2 large eggs
1/4 cup (60 g) butter, melted
2/3 cup (150 ml) milk
1/3 cup (50 g) cooked peas
1/3 cup (50 g) canned corn (sweetcorn)
2/3 cup (90 g) ham, diced

Pesto Muffins
with pine nuts

Preheat the oven to 350°F (180°C/gas 4). • Butter a 12-cup muffin pan. • Chop the basil and oil in a food processor until smooth. • Sift the flour, baking powder, and salt into a medium bowl. Stir in the Parmesan. • Beat the eggs and yogurt in a large bowl with an electric mixer on medium speed. • With mixer on low, gradually add the dry ingredients, basil mixture, and pine nuts, beating until just combined. • Spoon the batter into the prepared pan. • Bake until well risen and springy to the touch, about 20 minutes. • Let cool slightly before turning out onto a wire rack.

Large bunch fresh basil
1/4 cup (60 ml) extra-virgin olive oil
1 2/3 cups (250 g) all-purpose (plain) flour
3 teaspoons baking powder
1/2 teaspoon salt
1/2 cup (60 g) freshly grated Parmesan
2 large eggs
1 cup (250 ml) plain yogurt
1/3 cup (60 g) pine nuts

MAKES about 12 muffins

PREPARATION 20 min

COOKING 30 min

DIFFICULTY level 1

Muffins

with feta and spinach

Preheat the oven to 350°F (180°C/gas 4). • Butter a 12-cup muffin pan. • Cook the spinach in a little lightly salted water over medium heat until tender, about 5 minutes. Drain well, squeezing out excess moisture. Chop finely. • Sift the flour, baking powder, and salt into a medium bowl. • Beat the eggs, oil, and yogurt in a large bowl with an electric mixer on medium speed until smooth. • With mixer on low, gradually add the dry ingredients, beating until just combined. • Stir in the spinach and feta by hand. • Spoon the batter into the prepared pan. • Bake until well risen and springy to the touch, about 20 minutes. • Let cool slightly before turning out onto a wire rack.

8 oz (250 g) fresh or frozen spinach

2⅓ cups (350 g) all-purpose (plain) flour

3 teaspoons baking powder

½ teaspoon salt

2 large eggs

¼ cup (60 ml) extra-virgin olive oil

1 cup (250 ml) natural yogurt

8 oz (250 g) Feta cheese, cut into small cubes

MAKES about 16 muffins

PREPARATION 15 min

COOKING 20 min

DIFFICULTY level 1

Muffins
with black olives

Preheat the oven to 350°F (180°C/gas 4). • Butter three 6-cup muffin pans. • Sift the flour, baking powder, and salt into a medium bowl. • Beat the eggs, oil, milk, herbs, and saffron in a large bowl with an electric mixer on medium speed until smooth. • With mixer on low, gradually add the dry ingredients, beating until just combined. • Stir in the olives in by hand. • Spoon the batter into the prepared pan. Top each muffin with a whole olive. • Bake until well risen and springy to the touch, about 20 minutes. • Let cool slightly before turning out onto a wire rack.

2⅓ cups (350 g) all-purpose (plain) flour
2 teaspoons baking powder
½ teaspoon salt
3 large eggs
½ cup (125 ml) extra-virgin olive oil
1 cup (250 ml) milk
1 teaspoon Provençal herbs
Pinch of saffron strands
Scant 1½ cups (150 g) pitted black olives, coarsely chopped + 16 whole olives, to garnish

Parmesan Muffins
with fresh thyme

Preheat the oven to 350°F (180°C/gas 4). • Butter a 12-cup muffin pan. • Sift the flour, baking powder, and salt into a medium bowl. Stir in the Parmesan. • Beat the eggs, oil, yogurt, and thyme in a large bowl with an electric mixer on medium speed until smooth. • With mixer on low, gradually add the dry ingredients, beating until just combined. • Spoon the batter into the prepared pan. • Bake until well risen and springy to the touch, about 20 minutes. • Let cool slightly before turning out onto a wire rack.

- 1$\frac{2}{3}$ cups (250 g) all-purpose (plain) flour
- 2$\frac{1}{2}$ teaspoons baking powder
- $\frac{1}{2}$ teaspoon salt
- $\frac{2}{3}$ cup (100 g) freshly grated Parmesan
- 2 large eggs
- 2 tablespoons extra-virgin olive oil
- 1 cup (250 ml) plain yogurt
- 1 tablespoon finely chopped thyme

MAKES about 12 muffins

PREPARATION 15 min

COOKING 20 min

DIFFICULTY level 1

Cheese Muffins
with zucchini

Preheat the oven to 350°F (180°C/gas 4). • Butter a 12-cup muffin pan. • Grate the zucchini and then squeeze gently to remove excess liquid. • Sift the flour, baking powder, and salt into a medium bowl. • Beat the eggs, oil, and milk in a large bowl with an electric mixer at medium speed until smooth. • With mixer on low, gradually add the dry ingredients, beating until just combined. • Put the goat cheese into a bowl and mix with a fork to make a smooth cream. Stir the zucchini, pine nuts, and goat cheese into the egg mixture. • Spoon the batter into the prepared pan. • Bake until well risen and springy to the touch, about 20 minutes. • Let cool slightly before turning out onto a wire rack.

2 large zucchini (courgettes)
2 cups (300 g) all-purpose (plain) flour
3 teaspoons baking powder
$\frac{1}{2}$ teaspoon salt
2 large eggs
$\frac{1}{2}$ cup (125 ml) extra-virgin olive oil
$\frac{2}{3}$ cup (150 ml) milk
8 oz (250 g) fresh creamy goat cheese
$\frac{1}{4}$ cup (45 g) pine nuts

Index

Aniseed muffins with pine nuts, 29

Apple muffins with raisins and ricotta cheese, 38

Apricot muffins, 4

Banana muffins with chocolate chips, 47

Blueberry muffins with white chocolate, 16

Carrot muffins with pine nuts, 39

Cheese muffins with zucchini, 62

Chocolate muffins with cherry and port topping, 20

Coconut muffins with chocolate and rum, 14

Desert muffins with chocolate and tropical coulis, 40

Fruit muffins with yogurt, 13

Ginger muffins with orange marmalade, 36

Jaffa muffins with orange liqueur, 10

Lime muffins with yogurt, 6

Marbled muffins, 8

Muffins with apricot and almonds, 26

Muffins with black olives, 60

Muffins with caramel sauce, 19

Muffins with carrots and goat cheese, 55

Muffins with cashews and pears, 30

Muffins with chocolate and chile, 25

Muffins with coconut and cranberry, 18

Muffins with feta and spinach, 58

Muffins with ginger, pear, and chocolate, 22

Muffins with ham, peas, and corn, 56

Muffins with honey and thyme, 50

Muffins with mandarins and chocolate, 12

Muffins with bacon and hazelnuts, 54

Muffins with passionfruit and mango, 48

Muffins with pears and pecans, 32

Muffins with prunes and walnuts, 9

Muffins with strawberry sauce, 49

Mufins with cherries and almonds, 44

Nutty muffins with yogurt and spice, 28

Orange muffins with sticky orange sauce, 5

Parmesan muffins with fresh thyme, 61

Pesto muffins with pine nuts, 57

Rice muffins, 42

Rose muffins with almonds, 35

Zucchini muffins with lime frosting, 52

Copyright © 2007 by McRae Books Srl

This English edition first published in 2007

Text: Carla Bardi

Editing: Osla Fraser

Photography: Cristina Canepari, Keeho Casati, Gil Gallo, Walter Mericchi, Sandra Preussinger

Home Economist: Benedetto Rillo

Artbuying: McRae Books

Layouts: Adina Stefania Dragomir

Repro: Fotolito Raf, Florence

All rights reserved. No part of this book may be reproduced in any form without the prior written permission of the publisher and copyright owner.

Muffins

was created and produced by McRae Books Srl

Borgo Santa Croce, 8 – Florence (Italy)

info@mcraebooks.com

Publishers: Anne McRae and Marco Nardi

Project Director: Anne McRae

Design: Sara Mathews

ISBN 978-88-89272-86-2

Printed and bound in China